Vocabulary questions feature heavily on 11+ exams and other selective tests. This prac developed with this in mind and contains a range of questions that have been set on re in this book will help foster confidence in children and boost their vocabulary knowled; regular reading of a variety of books is one of the most effective ways to build a child's

How to use this resource:

There are sixteen types of exercises within this book. Children are encouraged to use appropriate dictionaries, thesauruses, apps and websites that are available to them to help them learn the meanings of new words and to be able to identify synonyms and antonyms for each word. They should not simply be guessing answers.

Each exercise has instructions at the top. Some of these instruct children to choose the answer from the choices, which they can circle, underline, etc. Others have a line on which children can write their answer. Children may want to tick or cross off words that have already been used within certain exercises. After every tenth exercise in this book, you will find a log for recording words from the exercises that were unfamiliar to the child, and there is space to also record definitions, synonyms, and antonyms for each of the unfamiliar words. Children could also use their own books, paper, or index cards to record these. It would aid in their retention of new vocabulary, and children would then be more likely to use new words within their own writing. An example of each type of question covered in this practice book is given below to show how each type of exercise should be completed.

Below are examples of each type of exercise:

Definitions

Select the correct word for each of the following definitions. Each word can be used only once.

wait	artful	colour	limb	paid
change	box ✔	neat	idol	rare

___box___ : a container, usually rectangular, of wood, etc., and often with a lid or cover (noun)

Synonyms

Choose one word from the five options which means the same or nearly the same as the bold word on the left.

quiet	loud	start	meal	(calm)	noise

Antonyms

Choose one word from the five options which means the opposite or nearly the opposite as the bold word on the left.

loud	courageous	(silent)	rowdy	roaring	short

Word connections

Three of the words in each list are connected to each other. Circle the word which does not belong.

banana	orange	apple	(carrot)

Carrot is a vegetable; the rest are fruit.

Similar Meanings

Fill in the missing letters to find the word with a similar meaning to the one in bold.

odd – st <u>r</u> <u>a</u> <u>n</u> <u>g</u> <u>e</u>

Word Categories

Look at the word on the left. Circle the category on the right that the word belongs to.

ketchup	drink	meal	(condiment)	soup

Similarities

Circle the word from the choices that is the best synonym for the word in bold and makes sense in the sentence.

The two people had a heated **dispute** which was very quickly resolved.

(argument)	peace	harmony	stove

Words Which Do Not Match

Circle the word from the choices that does not match the word in bold. There is only one best answer.

money	coins	cash	currency	(table)

Double Meanings

Circle the word outside the brackets that has a similar meaning to the words in both sets of brackets.

(ability   talent)   (offering   present)   **skill   (gift)   bonus   genius**

Opposite Meanings

Fill in the missing letters to find the word with the opposite meaning to the one in bold.

unite – dis <u>c</u> <u>o</u> nn <u>e</u> <u>c</u> <u>t</u>

Find the Missing Word

Circle the word which would best fit into the sentence.

1. I took a _____ to learn about flower arrangement.

   (course)   study   coarse   floral

Sorting Synonymous Words

Put the words in the box into the correct column to list the synonyms for 'good' and for 'bad.'

great	dreadful
inferior	positive

Good	Bad
great	inferior
positive	dreadful

Pairs of Synonyms

Select the word from the box that is the **synonym** of the word on the left.

lengthy	...	...	...	...
...	...	...	...	...

long   ____ lengthy ____

Pairs of Antonyms

Select the word from the box that is the **antonym** of the word on the left.

short	...	...	...	...
...	...	...	...	...

tall   ____ short ____

Homophones

Circle the correct homophone to complete the sentence on the left.

The lovely scent of the apple trees filled the _____.   heir   (air)

Compound Words

Circle one word from each set of brackets which form a compound word.

(bar (can) see)   (less   end (not))   *The word is ____ **cannot** ____.*

Exercise 1 – Definitions

Select the correct word for each of the following definitions. Each word can be used only once.

perplexed	orthodontics	ignorant	fatigue	resort
covert	submissive	adhere	condemn	lament

1. _____ : to stick to something, to attach firmly to something (verb)

2. _____ : not openly acknowledged or displayed (adj)

3. _____ : a branch of dentistry that deals with helping teeth to grow straight (noun)

4. _____ : to express sorrow, regret, or unhappiness about something (verb)

5. _____ : not having enough knowledge, understanding, or information about something (adj)

6. _____ : extreme tiredness or exhaustion (noun)

7. _____ : willing to obey someone else (adj)

8. _____ : to do or use (something) because no other choices are possible (verb)

9. _____ : unable to understand something clearly or think clearly (adj)

10. _____ : to criticise something or someone very strongly, usually for moral reasons (verb)

Exercise 2 – Synonyms

Choose one word from the five options which means the same or nearly the same as the bold word on the left.

1. **perceive**   observe   receive   sedate   person   remember

2. **retreat**   engage   depart   treat   image   fresh

3. **shrink**   bored   polite   babble   expand   diminish

4. **commence**   sew   initiate   handy   method   scruffy

5. **despise**   chuckle   consent   abhor   patient   blend

6. **reveal**   separate   notice   foremost   disclose   hide

7. **rowdy**   break   mute   unruly   begin   erroneous

8. **pretence**   deceit   honesty   tense   apt   eager

9. **perish**   build   swell   expire   shrewd   weaken

10. **conceit**   pride   simmer   shiny   taut   resistant

Riddle Time!

Q : What gets sharper the more you use it?

A : *Your brain.*

Exercise 3 – Antonyms

Choose one word from the five options which means the opposite or nearly the opposite as the bold word on the left.

1. **lofty**   minuscule   tall   endure   invade   mature

2. **nauseous**   naughty   constant   select   sick   soothed

3. **tempestuous** continue   worse   stormy   calm   tempt

4. **endure**   surrender   persist   antic   violent   guilty

5. **deceit**   fraud   peace   obscure   honesty   astute

6. **wither**   implore   weather   chide   decay   flourish

7. **volatile**   stable   hostile   weary   violin   vibrate

8. **nimble**   numb   clumsy   rapid   accuse   agile

9. **conceal**   divulge   hide   bustle   sincere   contorted

10. **superfluous** confine   useful   scorn   extra   subtle

Keep Up The Good Work

THE LEAPING LEARNER

THE LEAPING LEARNER

Exercise 4 – Word connections

Three of the words in each list are connected to each other. Circle the word which does not belong.

1. negligent   careless   careful   inattentive

2. peril   jeopardy   security   hazard

3. perilous   calm   composure   tranquillity

4. inflexible   lenient   unbending   unwavering

5. derelict   restored   dilapidated   ramshackle

6. repel   coax   cajole   persuade

7. discourse   speech   sermon   lesson

8. restrained   emotional   mild   nonchalant

9. common   bizarre   odd   peculiar

10. toil   effort   passivity   endeavour

Exercise 5 – Find the Missing Word

Circle the word which would best fit into the sentence.

1. The criminal had been a known _____ offender.

   cereal   **serial**   **sequence**   **several**

2. The professor is renowned for being one of the most _____ speakers in the world.

   instantaneous   **disassociated**   **charismatic**   **good**

3. The children were looking forward to visiting the _____ of their new school.

   cite   **sight**   **site**   **house**

4. The classroom was extremely hot during the summer; the _____ focus was hindered.

   children   **crowd's**   **child**   **children's**

5. There was a terrible accident; she had damaged her spinal _____.

   chord   **cord**   **cored**   **core**

6. She worked hard to get her results and everyone paid her many _____.

   compliments   **complacent**   **money**   **complements**

7. The child enjoyed learning how machines work; he _____ them to see inside.

   disassembled   **resembled**   **assembled**   **assembly**

8. The surface of sandpaper is very _____, which makes it very useful in woodwork.

   course   **cores**   **coarse**   **chores**

9. The man tried very hard not to _____ his temper when the shop worker was rude to him.

   loose   **dislocate**   **find**   **lose**

10. He used the photos he took to make a _____ for his parents' anniversary gift.

    college   **collect**   **selection**   **collage**

Riddle Time!

Q : What word is spelled wrong in every dictionary?

A : _The word "wrong."_

THE LEAPING LEARNER   THE LEAPING LEARNER

Exercise 6 – Opposite Meanings

Fill in the missing letters to find the word with the opposite meaning to the one in **bold**.

1. **rare**   com __ __ n

2. **temporary**   pe __ __ an __ __ t

3. **amateur**   p__ __ ffe __ __ __ __ __ al

4. **graceful**   aw __ __ a __ d

5. **tranquil**   bois __ __ __ o __ __

6. **frugal**   ext __ __ __ __ __ __ nt

7. **lucky**   unf __ __ __ __ __ __ __ e

8. **plentiful**   sc __ __ __ e

9. **incarcerate**   lib __ __ __ __ e

10. **question**   res __ __ __ __ __

Exercise 7 – Pairs of Synonyms

Select the word from the box that is the synonym of the word on the left.

confidential	shorten	relish	chore	roam
peddle	commodity	bloated	callous	onerous

1. swollen   _____

2. product   _____

3. sell   _____

4. delight   _____

5. heartless   _____

6. assignment   _____

7. private   _____

8. laborious   _____

9. abbreviate   _____

10. meander   _____

Exercise 8 – Word Categories

Look at the word on the left. Circle the category on the right that the word belongs to.

1. **sanitary**   dirty   hygiene   garish   funny

2. **fertile**   colour   language   park   productive

3. **regret**   sorrow   health   measure   animals

4. **inhabitants**   food   occupants   doctor   shapes

5. **wretched**   tragic   happiness   cities   books

6. **emulate**   parts   imitate   roads   rivers

7. **tranquil**   restless   wishes   serene   places

8. **trivial**   games   problems   parties   unimportant

9. **deny**   forbid   acceptance   sever   hostile

10. **flamboyant**   modesty   authors   dazzling   famine

Exercise 9 – Similarities

Circle the word from the choices that is the best synonym for the word in bold and makes sense in the sentence.

1. The black cat **vanished** into the night.
    materialised   disappeared   jotted   waited

2. They went through an **arduous** training program.
    benevolent   complete   laborious   deep

3. She **frivolously** spent her money.
    swiftly   repeatedly   gracefully   thoughtlessly

4. They loved the beautiful, **quaint** cottage.
    foul   rotten   verifiable   picturesque

5. He was extremely **resolute** with his decision to leave his job.
    determined   feeble   vexed   petrified

6. The king would **banish** any person who dared oppose him.
    nourish   compliment   douse   extradite

7. I am feeling **apprehensive** about the exam I have to write next week.
    composed   exuberant   inundated   doubtful

8. Clara seemed **sincere** in her commitment to finishing the project.
    genuine   devious   erratic   renewed

9. He expressed his **gratitude** to everyone who helped him.
    ungratefulness   jealousy   appreciation   uncertainty

10. She gave a clear and **factual** statement about the incident to the detectives.
    negligent   repetitive   credible   hilarious

Riddle Time!

Q : What word contains 26 letters, but only three syllables?

A : _Alphabet!_

Exercise 10 – Words Which Do Not Match

Circle the word from the choices that does not match the word in bold. There is only one best answer.

1. **stoop**   crouch   bow   sink   straighten

2. **placid**   serene   agitated   tranquil   quiet

3. **distinct**   obscure   clear   noticeable   definite

4. **defy**   flout   disregard   assist   confront

5. **oath**   pledge   testimony   vow   silence

6. **triumph**   pride   failure   elation   celebration

7. **virtue**   evil   ethics   morality   integrity

8. **allure**   charm   glamour   repel   appeal

9. **majestic**   grand   dignified   marvellous   shabby

10. **subdue**   release   tame   quell   defeat

Great Job

Have you come across any unfamiliar words in the last 10 exercises?
There is space below for you to write the words down, their definitions,
synonyms, and antonyms:

Word	Definition	Synonyms	Antonyms

Exercise 11 – Definitions

Select the correct word for each of the following definitions. Each word can be used only once.

humdrum	berate	novice	primate	ransack
format	midriff	earmark	steadfast	pretend

1. _____ : to put something aside for a particular purpose (verb)

2. _____ : the size and shape of something (noun)

3. _____ : to scold or criticize someone harshly (verb)

4. _____ : a beginner (noun)

5. _____ : firm; not changing one's aims or attitudes (adj)

6. _____ : to appear falsely in order to deceive someone (verb)

7. _____ : go hurriedly through a place stealing, causing damage and leaving a mess (verb)

8. _____ : an animal of the group including monkeys and apes (noun)

9. _____ : the front part of the body between the chest and waist (noun)

10. _____ : not exciting; dull (adj)

Exercise 12 – Synonyms

Choose one word from the five options which means the same or nearly the same as the bold word on the left.

1. **assign**   reject   appoint   literature   herd   detail

2. **candid**   artful   colourful   slight   blunt   hoarse

3. **shipshape**   messy   misshapen   tardy   short   tidy

4. **leeward**   sheltered   amazed   mistaken   tired   late

5. **offspring**   elderly   young   parent   adult   source

6. **deadpan**   warm   liked   impassive   heroic   spiked

7. **paddock**   lock   trickery   field   untidy   elongated

8. **yield**   debt   profit   tirade   steep   varied

9. **feign**   sincere   joyous   elite   tired   sham

10. **immerse**   engage   reject   tall   ignore   sealed

Exercise 13 – Antonyms

Choose one word from the five options which means the opposite as the bold word on the left.

1. **arid**   damp   parched   vivid   rotten   hope

2. **shun**   stroke   deceive   accept   wait   destroy

3. **lenient**   pristine   erase   vital   bored   intolerant

4. **current**   outdated   modern   leased   deployed   correct

5. **excavate**   cover   understand   dilute   treachery   benign

6. **evasive**   translucent   tight   frank   evade   delayed

7. **pedestrian**   dull   delighted   extraordinary   opposite   bouncy

8. **scheduled**   airy   untrue   elastic   disorganised   rough

9. **dwindle**   diminish   reduce   expand   distress   titled

10. **disperse**   align   scatter   revise   collect   embolden

Riddle Time!

Q : What building has thousands of stories?

A : _The library!_

Exercise 14 – Word connections

Three of the words in each list are connected to each other. Circle the word which does not belong.

1.   concerned   apprehensive   uneasy   charred

2.   trapped   rural   besieged   blockade

3.   palpable   obvious   murky   evident

4.   ignited   dilapidated   derelict   damaged

5.   skyward   lofty   towering   delicious

6.   flexible   lenient   quaint   liberal

7.   prominent   tranquil   renowned   famed

8.   erratic   unpredictable   youthful   unstable

9.   solid   puzzled   perplexed   uncertain

10.   imprudent   absurd   ridiculous   obliged

Keep Going

Exercise 15 – Find the Missing Word

Circle the word which would best fit into the sentence.

1. I had to take a _____ of antibiotics to treat an infection.

   coarse   class   course   bunch

2. My mentor gave me some fantastic _____ about how to begin my project.

   advise   counsel   advice   discouragement

3. As a food critic, he assures me that he has a discernible _____.

   pallet   palate   pellet   palliate

4. The nurse had some trouble finding a _____ during his blood donation.

   vane   vain   vine   vein

5. They made a _____ to do the work together as a group.

   pact   packed   impact   pace

6. The family was _____ the loss of their pet cat.

   morning   rejoicing   mourning   delighting

7. She is known to have a very forceful _____ of speaking.

   manor   manna   wrong   manner

8. They needed to repair the _____ on the bicycle before resuming their journey.

   peddle   petal   pendant   pedal

9. The cake recipe requires the _____ from several eggs, among other ingredients.

   yoke   yolk   omelette   exterior

10. The waves on the beach gently _____ during low tide.

    reseed   receive   recede   rise

Exercise 16 – Similar Meanings

Fill in the missing letters to find the word with a similar meaning to the one in bold.

1. **affable**   so __ __ __ __ le

2. **covet**   c __ __ __ e

3. **latter**   f __ __ __ l

4. **feeble**   ina __ __ __ __ __ te

5. **restrain**   sup __ __ __ __ s

6. **emerge**   un __ __ __ d

7. **polarity**   con __ __ __ ct

8. **painstaking**   ca __ __ f __ l

9. **idiosyncrasy**   t __ __ it

10. **conflagration**   wi __ d __ __ re

Riddle Time!

Q : What five-letter word gets shorter when you add two letters to it?

A : _Short._

Exercise 17 – Opposite Meanings

Fill in the missing letters to find the word with the opposite meaning to the one in bold.

1. **quell**   __ e __ p

2. **robust**   del __ __ a __ e

3. **succumb**   r __ s __ s __

4. **unorthodox**   __ __ nven __ ion __ l

5. **matte**   g __ o __ __ y

6. **obstinate**   com __ l __ an __

7. **vicarious**   mer __ il __ ss

8. **temperate**   e __ tre __ __

9. **vacant**   oc __ __ pi __ __

10. **public**   __ ri __ a __ e

Exercise 18 – Homophones

Circle the correct homophone to complete the sentence on the left.

1. I made the _____ as tight as I could.   **naught**   **knot**

2. You must _____ dough very well to make bread.   **need**   **knead**

3. There is a cottage at the _____ of the mountain.   **peek**   **peak**

4. She gave him advice which made a lot of _____.   **sense**   **scents**

5. Take hold of the _____ to control the horse!   **reigns**   **reins**

6. Would you prefer a _____ or a banana?   **pear**   **pare**

7. There is a lovely _____ tree in their garden.   **ewe**   **yew**

8. The eagle _____ on small mammals.   **praise**   **preys**

9. The building _____ has been cleared for safety.   **cite**   **site**

10. A pickup truck has _____ the vehicle away.   **toed**   **towed**

Keep Going

Exercise 19 – Similarities

Circle the word from the choices that is the best synonym for the word in bold and makes sense in the sentence.

1.   There is no **repository** in which to store trains.

   apartment   cabin   case   depot

2.   With all of the **clutter**, her room was in a state of disarray.

   neatness   untidiness   enlargement   consolation

3.   People who are hermits live away from society, in **isolation**.

   solitude   civilization   public   revolution

4.   The witness in the trial experienced much **torment** from the lawyer's questioning.

   pleasantry   banter   resentment   distress

5.   Seeing a mountain lion on their path **roused** a sense of fear in the tourists.

   decreased   frightened   anticipated   awakened

6.   The bird flew to its nest under the bridge to feed its **brood**.

   young   group   separate   litter

7.   There was a lot of **coarse** sand covering the beach.

   soft   polite   rough   miniature

8.   Carrots must be **grated** to make a carrot cake.

   moulded   shredded   twisted   curled

9.   Having woken up late, John was **bewildered** as he rushed into school that morning.

   perplexed   jocular   elite   certain

10. **Convicts** in prison must follow a very strict schedule.

   wardens   victims   citizens   prisoners

Exercise 20 – Compound Words

Circle one word from each set of brackets to form a compound word. The first part of the compound word will be in the first set of brackets.

1. (water   disc   fly)   (fall   hard   ton)   The word is _____.

2. (stage   enter   teal)   (into   prise   ring)   The word is _____.

3. (bead   heed   bed)   (rag   rock   stone)   The word is _____.

4. (accept   plot   tree)   (age   ants   able)   The word is _____.

5. (and   red   back)   (dive   drop   deer)   The word is _____.

6. (brow   tint   since)   (ring   sing   sure)   The word is _____.

7. (him   feat   sent)   (her   sure   path)   The word is _____.

8. (super   adult   right)   (tend   rite   natural)   The word is _____.

9. (brake   set   sort)   (back   through   down)   The word is _____.

10. (no   sheet   sum)   (were   bodied   thing)   The word is _____.

Riddle Time!

Q : How many letters are there in the English alphabet?

A : _Eighteen! 3 in 'the', 7 in 'English,' and 8 in 'alphabet.'_

Have you come across any unfamiliar words in the last 10 exercises?
There is space below for you to write the words down, their definitions,
synonyms, and antonyms:

Word	Definition	Synonyms	Antonyms

THE LEAPING LEARNER

THE LEAPING LEARNER

Exercise 21 – Definitions

Select the correct word for each of the following definitions. Each word can be used only once.

inaugural	companion	pigment	plume	meticulous
asunder	errand	arduous	tempestuous	consent

1. _____ : a colouring matter or substance (noun)

2. _____ : permission, approval, or agreement (noun)

3. _____ : taking or showing extreme care about small details (adj)

4. _____ : a short and quick trip to accomplish a specific purpose (noun)

5. _____ : separated or split into parts (adj)

6. _____ : marking the beginning of a new venture (adj)

7. _____ : a mate, friend or a match for something (noun)

8. _____ : tumultuous or turbulent (adj)

9. _____ : a soft, fluffy feather (noun)

10. _____ : requiring great exertion; difficult (adj)

THE LEAPING LEARNER

THE LEAPING LEARNER

Exercise 22 – Synonyms

Choose one word from the five options which means the same or nearly the same as the bold word on the left.

1. **adopt**   deny   adapt   accept   lacking   forced

2. **broad**   limited   lessened   retrieval   loaned   extensive

3. **fabricate**   genuine   fabric   unneeded   delayed   falsify

4. **venerable**   esteemed   compliant   endanger   slow   unimpressive

5. **oppress**   subdue   change   suppress   excite   reveal

6. **gregarious**   tall   smooth   unfriendly   sociable   entitled

7. **intangible**   obvious   delighted   serene   zeal   untouchable

8. **ramble**   ample   excursion   rapid   beverage   importance

9. **traitor**   loyalist   elector   betrayer   assignment   meander

10. **liberty**   dependence   natural   fame   subjugation   autonomy

Exercise 23 – Antonyms

Choose one word from the five options which means the opposite as the bold word on the left.

1. **presume**   assume   constraint   doubt   trust   <u>halt</u>

2. **elegant**   <u>gauche</u>   charm   disbelief   politeness   intense

3. **seldom**   pleased   rarely   receipt   often   vendor

4. **infinite**   endless   <u>ceasing</u>   aloft   severe   elated

5. **raucous**   harsh   descriptive   elite   subpar   calm

6. **cantankerous**   ideal   strident   affable   justice   credit

7. **odious**   delightful   repulsive   lonely   origin   <u>obvious</u>

8. **camaraderie**   distinction   harmony   vague   animosity   clarity

9. **conclude**   complete   release   combine   ultimate   <u>commence</u>

10. **promote**   ease   improve   probe   boost   <u>demote</u>

Riddle Time!

Q : Which weighs more: a pound of feathers or a pound of bricks?

A : <u>*They weigh the same.*</u>

Exercise 24 – Find the Missing Word

Circle the word which would best fit into the sentence.

1. The walls of the castle had been _____ over the years to a higher standard.
    sent   positioned   renovated   broken

2. Ava was completely _____ with the coursework for her new class.
    fascinated   scowled   undermined   fought

3. His artwork won the prestigious award, but I thought it was quite _____.
    flat   mediocre   amicable   mustered

4. Her written work was completely _____ and she received full marks for it.
    flawed   hilarious   precise   haughty

5. Paul was overcome with _____ and needed to rest immediately.
    vigour   objection   amusement   exhaustion

6. They found doing the same lessons every day to be highly _____.
    full   wary   monotonous   gifted

7. He gave his mother a very _____ card which made her emotional.
    sentimental   bashful   negligent   adequate

8. The structure became very _____ after the flooding and was deemed dangerous.
    sturdy   unsound   watertight   uninspiring

9. Sally has an _____ to swimming due to her fear of water.
    pride   account   inability   aversion

10. They had to _____ the meeting due to an emergency in another part of the building.
    rejuvenate   detail   ignore   curtail

You are learning so many new words!

Exercise 25 – Similar Meanings

Fill in the missing letters to find the word with a similar meaning to the one in bold.

1. **cordial**   fr __ __ __ __ ly

2. **home**   ha __ __ __ __ t

3. **liberate**   re __ __ __ __ __

4. **humid**   m __ __ __ t

5. **correspond**   com __ __ __ __ __ __ te

6. **heroic**   b __ __ __ __

7. **flare**   f __ __ __ h

8. **residue**   re __ __ __ __ __ er

9. **lucid**   we __ __ -sp __ __ __ n

10. **orator**   sp __ __ __ __ r

Exercise 26 – Sorting Synonymous Words

Put the words in the box into the correct column to list the synonyms for 'simple' and for 'complex.'

intricate	elementary	facile	plain
complicated	straightforward	challenging	direct
effortless	perplexing	uncomplicated	confusing
difficult	basic	involved	convoluted
cinch	arduous	clear	elaborate

Simple	Complex

Exercise 27 – Pairs of Synonyms

Select the word from the box that is the synonym of the word on the left.

flippant	fluctuate	impartial	defy	instinctive
imitate	permeate	sustain	bedlam	haughty

1. continue _____

2. penetrate _____

3. violate _____

4. facetious _____

5. alternate _____

6. neutral _____

7. intuitive _____

8. mimic _____

9. pandemonium _____

10. pompous _____

Riddle Time!

Q : What 7 letter word is spelled the same way backwards and forwards?

A : _Racecar._

Exercise 28 – Word Categories

Look at the word on the left. Circle the category on the right that the word belongs to.

1. **emerald**   species   stone   shop   car

2. **architect**   doctor   builder   designer   care

3. **beverage**   meal   drink   clothes   accessory

4. **burrow**   shelter   workplace   instrument   tool

5. **dialogue**   silence   drawing   machine   conversation

6. **cuisine**   cooking   housing   dance   music

7. **saunter**   adverb   sewing   walk   holiday

8. **pedigree**   occupation   ancestry   reptile   device

9. **philanthropy**   paper   vehicle   charity   room

10. **adaptation**   adjustment   trial   roadway   herbs

Exercise 29 – Words Which Do Not Match

Circle the word from the choices that does not match the word in bold. There is only one best answer.

1. **dismiss**   fire   discharge   hire   oust   remove

2. **gemstone**   amethyst   diamond   opal   pearl   silver

3. **organ**   kidney   rib   heart   liver   skin

4. **fowl**   chicken   raven   grouse   pheasant   turkey

5. **pessimistic**   bleak   despondent   glum   optimistic   cynical

6. **skill**   art   prowess   learner   expertise   finesse

7. **monarchy**   princess   mayor   queen   prince   king

8. **dwelling**   apartment   bungalow   flat   shed   cottage

9. **bold**   audacious   daring   intrepid   gusty   vigilant

10. **crockery**   teacup   plate   saucer   spoon   bowl

Exercise 30 – Double Meanings

Circle the word outside the brackets that has a similar meaning to the words in both sets of brackets.

1. (point   direct)   (purpose   intention)   motive guide aim end

2. (stone   boulder)   (swing   sway)   cobble tilt rock roll

3. (fasten   bolt)   (curl   ringlet)   lock seal plait hair

4. (law   code)   (lead   reign)   push rule instruct order

5. (following   after)   (overdue   late)   behind delay next detain

6. (breeze   gale)   (reel   coil)   wind twist spiral blow

7. (purpose   use)   (event   party)   job ball function social

8. (error   fault)   (muddle   blunder)   baffle vague obscure mistake

9. (difficult   awkward)   (solid   firm)   complex hard stiff rigid

10. (recline   rest)   (deception   untruth)   lounge fake repose lie

What a workout !

Have you come across any unfamiliar words in the last 10 exercises?
There is space below for you to write the words down, their definitions,
synonyms, and antonyms:

Word	Definition	Synonyms	Antonyms

Exercise 31 – Definitions

Select the correct word for each of the following definitions. Each word can be used only once.

pompous	hoax	instantaneous	punctual	bargain
contract	admission	robust	divinity	privilege

1. _____ : being strictly observant of an appointed or regular time; prompt (adj)

2. _____ : a deity or diving being (noun)

3. _____ : something intended to deceive or defraud (noun)

4. _____ : an agreement enforceable by law (noun)

5. _____ : to be characterised by boastfulness and self-importance (adj)

6. _____ : the act of allowing to enter (noun)

7. _____ : a grant to an individual of a special right under certain conditions (noun)

8. _____ : something occurring or done without delay (adj)

9. _____ : a purchase acquired at less than the usual cost (noun)

10. _____ : strong and healthy (adj)

Exercise 32 – Synonyms

Choose one word from the five options which means the same or nearly the same as the bold word on the left.

1. **committee**   home   table   panel   breech   law

2. **vocation**   career   hobby   holiday   vocal   mural

3. **apparel**   appoint   parallel   plaits   towels   clothing

4. **façade**   fake   dormant   reality   person   cookery

5. **proportion**   imbalance   peak   trait   likeable   distribution

6. **grotesque**   beautiful   prime   gross   alien   serious

7. **inaudible**   loud   searching   awesome   muffled   inept

8. **sober**   irrational   forceful   lowly   tardy   solemn

9. **vacant**   full   popular   empty   lame   historical

10. **merchant**   trader   customer   shop   currency   busy

Riddle Time!

Q : What 4-letter word can be written forward,
backward or upside down, and can still be read from left to right?

A : _NOON_

Exercise 33 – Antonyms

Choose one word from the five options which means the opposite as the bold word on the left.

1. **obscure**   baffled   flagged   meandered   clarify   stood

2. **conflate**   meld   separate   confess   learn   deposit

3. **debate**   deliberate   harmonise   speech   bate   contour

4. **absurd**   abundant   ludicrous   bright   rational   leaky

5. **confine**   constrain   erase   await   congeal   release

6. **immerse**   ascend   steep   innate   spry   caked

7. **disarray**   unsettle   disorganise   display   retreat   organised

8. **clemency**   cruelty   disguise   compassion   temper   clergy

9. **destitute**   design   certain   affluent   needy   pretend

10. **endeavour**   strive   allow   strike   achieve   inactivity

Exercise 34 – Word connections

Three of the words in each list are connected to each other. Circle the word which does not belong.

1.   firefighter   teacher   doctor   (hospital)

2.   emergency   disaster   (suffering)   crisis

3.   (covenant)   vow   proclaim   pledge   *proclaim*

4.   easel   paint   (artist)   brush

5.   beverage   (bowl)   appetiser   dessert

6.   gloves   (sandals)   scarf   hat

7.   (wok)   knife   spoon   fork

8.   (saunter)   dash   sprint   jog

9.   novel   (author)   magazine   newspaper

10.   apartment   cottage   domicile   (office)

You're growing
your vocabulary !

THE LEAPING LEARNER

THE LEAPING LEARNER

Exercise 35 – Opposite Meanings

Fill in the missing letters to find the word with the opposite meaning to the one in bold.

1. **distinguished**   ord __ n __ __ y

2. **frivolous**   ma __ u __ e

3. **volatile**   de __ en __ abl __

4. **dampen**   de __ ydr __ __ e

5. **robust**   fr __ g __ l __

6. **prominent**   in __ is __ bl __

7. **invalid**   rea __ on __ __ l __

8. **maintain**   de __ tr __ __

9. **temperate**   un __ lea __ an __

10. **punctual**   t __ r __ y

Exercise 36 – Pairs of Antonyms

Select the word from the box that is the antonym of the word on the left.

approval	convenient	incautious	melancholy	supreme
boycott	modest	disturbance	uncouth	fulfilling

1. support   _____

2. harmony   _____

3. sophisticated   _____

4. refusal   _____

5. euphoric   _____

6. dissatisfy   _____

7. prudent   _____

8. inferior   _____

9. conceited   _____

10. unhelpful   _____

Riddle Time!

Q : What English word has three consecutive double letters?

A : _Bookkeeper._

Exercise 37 – Homophones

Circle the correct homophone to complete the sentence on the left.

1. The lady mended the _____ on the garments for him.   **seam**   **seem**

2. I had to edit the _____ of my story before I submitted it.   **draught**   **draft**

3. He prepared an indulgent _____ for their dessert.   **moose**   **mousse**

4. The recipe called for several _____ of stock as a base.   **quartz**   **quarts**

5. A nurse puts a blood sample into a _____ for a blood test.   **vile**   **vial**

6. A _____ citizen holds a passport from two different countries.   **duel**   **dual**

7. Tom would rather have a _____ than an apple.   **plum**   **plumb**

8. The small child _____ after dropping her toy from the pram.   **bald**   **bawled**

9. There is too much at _____ to make risky decisions!   **stake**   **steak**

10. Teachers often need to _____ their lessons on the spot.   **alter**   **altar**

Exercise 38 – Similarities

Circle the word from the choices that is the best synonym for the word in bold and makes sense in the sentence.

1. The baby had **stirred** early in the morning, while her parents were still sleeping.
    awoken   wandered   slept   lingered

2. George realised he had broken his aunt's **priceless** vase.
    replaceable   useless   invaluable   feeble

3. The weather **deteriorated** throughout the night, and the wind thrashed the trees.
    soothed   increased   deposited   worsened

4. The driver was **reprimanded** by the traffic officer for speeding through the streets.
    commended   cautioned   praised   repaid

5. The children started to feel very **queasy** after eating too many of the sweets they had found.
    sickly   comfortable   healthy   extravagant

6. She was feeling **enthusiastic** to begin her new job working with animals.
    disappointed   ardent   sombre   stormy

7. When people grow older, their bones become much more **brittle**.
    durable   resilient   dormant   breakable

8. The animal skeleton found by the archaeologists was extremely **decomposed**.
    decayed   flourishing   perfumed   stingy

9. The man was known by many to be very **cunning** and sly.
    stupid   impartial   optimistic   crafty

10. The software programme had been **augmented** for better performance and usability.
    lessened   enhanced   reluctant   fibrous

Exercise 39 – Words Which Do Not Match

Circle the word from the choices that does not match the word in bold. There is only one best answer.

1. **oregano**   coriander   parsley   fennel   herbs   syrup

2. **facetious**   funny   comical   playful   angry   jocular

3. **stubborn**   adamant   headstrong   external   resolute   obstinate

4. **flair**   waste   skill   aptitude   talent   instinct

5. **ensign**   banner   flag   streamer   room   pennant

6. **diligent**   assiduous   lazy   industrious   persevering   tireless

7. **gawky**   clumsy   inept   lumbering   awkward   competent

8. **envelop**   uncover   surround   wrap   cocoon   encase

9. **acute**   intense   fierce   piercing   mild   sharp

10. **altitude**   distance   elevation   peak   summit   depth

THE LEAPING LEARNER   THE LEAPING LEARNER

Exercise 40 – Compound Words

Circle one word from each set of brackets which forms a compound word. The first part of the compound word will be in the first bracket.

1. (leaf   pass   try)   (port   end   den)   The word is _____.

2. (car   did   for)   (cup   mat   sea)   The word is _____.

3. (boil   ray   head)   (net   line   red)   The word is _____.

4. (pony   like   bar)   (see   tail   saw)   The word is _____.

5. (pass   lit   book)   (tie   look   mark)   The word is _____.

6. (any   face   run)   (where   were   sit)   The word is _____.

7. (cat   horse   shoe)   (back   float   pin)   The word is _____.

8. (ground   air   type)   (sit   plane   sin)   The word is _____.

9. (man   grand   flex)   (send   cent   son)   The word is _____.

10. (water   bench   fire)   (buy   fighter   leg)   The word is _____.

Have you come across any unfamiliar words in the last 10 exercises?
There is space below for you to write the words down, their definitions,
synonyms, and antonyms:

Word	Definition	Synonyms	Antonyms

Exercise 41 – Definitions

Select the correct word for each of the following definitions. Each word can be used only once.

grate	torment	promote	mere	wholly
segregation	immerse	suggest	vessel	odour

1. _____ : to mention or introduce an idea for consideration (verb)

2. _____ : to the whole or entire amount or extent (adv)

3. _____ : being nothing more nor better than (adj)

4. _____ : to plunge into or place under a liquid (verb)

5. _____ : a ship or boat; also a hollow utensil, such as a cup, used for holding liquid (noun)

6. _____ : a framework of metal bars used as a guard, partition, cover or the like (noun)

7. _____ : the action of setting someone or something apart from others (noun)

8. _____ : to help someone to flourish or go further (verb)

9. _____ : a sensation perceived by the sense of smell (noun)

10. _____ : to afflict with much bodily or mental suffering (verb)

Exercise 42 – Synonyms

Choose one word from the five options which means the same or nearly the same as the bold word on the left.

1. **antiquity** modern new antique comical below

2. **extinct** alive abolished exist comfort animal

3. **privilege** hinderance loss full season advantage

4. **income** revenue expenses bills outcome inept

5. **wound** content watery feeling joy damage

6. **stern** austere gentle light stem waiver

7. **rigid** soft rippled unmade calm stiff

8. **flee** flea arrive aware abscond wash

9. **coy** aggressive confident shy dry final

10. **category** group cattery sham shade link

Riddle Time!

Q : One word in this sentence is misspelled. What word is it?

A : _MISSPELLED. It isn't spelled wrong,_
the one word in this sentence IS "misspelled."

Exercise 43 – Antonyms

Choose one word from the five options which means the opposite or nearly the opposite as the bold word on the left.

1. **bargain**   deal   rip-off   barge   contest   level

2. **clemency**   mercy   clementine   menace   clearance   cruelty

3. **coax**   cajole   dissuade   hoax   soapy   press

4. **deliberate**   unintentional   careful   plan   debris   libel

5. **covet**   desire   cover   convent   dislike   spoil

6. **ally**   partner   alley   enemy   align   edgy

7. **chaos**   order   disarray   captive   free   tremulous

8. **ventilate**   vent   suppress   late   state   destitute

9. **resign**   continue   abandon   sign   contract   schedule

10. **slope**   lean   bend   scope   stamp   level

Exercise 44 – Find the Missing Word

Circle the word which would best fit into the sentence.

1. The _____ crowds flocking to the monument made for a very busy day in the shops nearby.

    calamitous   limpid   deficient   constant

2. The beautiful painting of the placid lake looks incredibly _____.

    nervous   serene   foolish   corpulent

3. The roses were a pale pink colour and the scent _____ across the garden.

    withdrew   emanated   twisted   screeched

4. The trainees were all feeling excited and _____ to begin their new careers.

    keen   disinterested   interesting   noteworthy

5. Lisa knew she needed to be more _____ and not spend all her money on shoes.

    uneconomical   frugal   impressed   loyal

6. The school curriculum takes much time and consideration to _____.

    decrease   gobble   erode   develop

7. Always have a plan, but be _____ and willing to adapt to new situations.

    resistant   noxious   flexible   ridiculous

8. Having been in the sun all day, Amir felt very hot and _____ by evening.

    parched   watered   misty   elated

9. Usually someone who has been doing a job for years is more _____ than a new recruit.

    inept   experienced   untrained   doltish

10. The students knew that their final days at school would be the most _____ so they wanted to make the most of them.

    memorable   reliable   sizeable   wrinkled

Exercise 45 – Similar Meanings

Fill in the missing letters to find the word with a similar meaning to the one in bold.

1. **intense**   fi __ rc __

2. **revive**   r __ n __ w

3. **raiment**   cl __ __ he __

4. **pattern**   arr __ __ ge __ e __ t

5. **provoke**   a __ g __ __

6. **system**   st __ uct __ __e

7. **limit**   ma __ i __ um

8. **option**   c __ __ i __ e

9. **flora**   p __ ant __

10. **expensive**   c __ st __ y

Check you out!
Keep up the awesome work!

Exercise 46 – Sorting Synonymous Words

Put the words in the box into the correct column to list the synonyms for 'light' and for 'heavy.'

buoyant	dainty	agile	burdensome
hefty	lightweight	beefy	luminosity
substantial	massive	flimsy	dense
slight	airy	lead-footed	bulky
weighty	considerable	floating	feathery

Light	Heavy

Exercise 47 – Word Categories

Look at the word on the left. Circle the category on the right that the word belongs to.

1. **confusion**   understanding   clarity   uncertainty   ancestry

2. **mammal**   gorilla   bird   insect   eggs

3. **ellipsis**   tool   writing   punctuation   comma

4. **dweller**   profession   inhabitant   animal   worker

5. **dialect**   words   speaking   accent   writing

6. **government**   politics   money   passport   records

7. **orchid**   bag   vegetable   colour   flower

8. **brother**   sibling   colleague   friend   comrade

9. **wrench**   mechanic   bolt   screwdriver   tool

10. **lemon**   citrus   vegetable   spice   herb

Riddle Time!

Q : What familiar word starts with IS, ends with AND, and has LA in the middle.

A : _ISLAND._

Exercise 48 – Similarities

Circle the word from the choices that is the best synonym for the word in bold and makes sense in the sentence.

1.   She knew she could never **betray** her friend's trust.
     forsake   limit   tighten   assist

2.   There was a **scarcity** of the equipment needed for the workers to be safe.
     excess   manage   lack   hidden

3.   There was an abundance of beautiful **flora** covering the countryside.
     stones   buildings   animals   vegetation

4.   The incident was clearly **calculated** and not an accident at all.
     solved   deliberate   distinct   partial

5.   Throughout the **calamity**, Ahmed managed to remain calm and collected.
     ordeal   comfort   guarantee   nuisance

6.   The **merchants** at the market displayed their lovely goods on the rows of tables.
     customers   buyers   consumers   vendors

7.   The **family** living in the residence were asked to participate in the survey.
     office   household   residents   industry

8.   At the swimming baths, many of the inflatable devices were **perforated**, and therefore ruined.
     punctured   sewn   attached   repaired

9.   The younger child **provoked** his older siblings by destroying their books on purpose.
     appeased   dissuaded   aggravated   trusted

10. She **recited** the poem beautifully, and the audience was astonished.
     withheld   suppressed   recounted   failed

Exercise 49 – Words Which Do Not Match

Circle the word from the choices that does not match the word in bold. There is only one best answer.

1. **exhibit**   show   display   hide   model

2. **hostile**   bitter   favourable   nasty   opposed

3. **boost**   support   bolster   maintain   undermine

4. **exploit**   cherish   use   manipulate   abuse

5. **pester**   tease   bother   badger   comfort

6. **convene**   assemble   gather   summon   adjourn

7. **enact**   approve   repeal   execute   perform

8. **revive**   energize   rejuvenate   revitalize   depress

9. **docile**   inflexible   meek   pliable   pliant

10. **refined**   classy   crass   elegant   tasteful

Exercise 50 – Double Meanings

Circle the word outside the brackets that has a similar meaning to the words in both sets of brackets.

1. (run   dash)   (tribe   people)   race   sprint   type   nation

2. (scratch   dent)   (grade   assess)   rate   cut   judge   mark

3. (pursue   hunt)   (route   path)   way   chase   track   passage

4. (abandon   dump)   (drain   trench)   leave   gutter   rubbish   ditch

5. (surrender   submit) (produce   crop)   supply   yield   surplus   comply

6. (straightforward   honest) (guide   control)   aim   steer   direct   open

7. (introduce   display) (gift   donation)   show   present   favour   prize

8. (obstacle   snag)   (seize   grab)   catch   clutch   difficulty   problem

9. (filling   load)   (happy   fulfilled)   content   packing   stuffed   great

10. (selfish   miserly) (middle   medium)   greedy   mean   nasty   stingy

Keep Up The Good Work !

Have you come across any unfamiliar words in the last 10 exercises?
There is space below for you to write the words down, their definitions,
synonyms, and antonyms:

Word	Definition	Synonyms	Antonyms

THE LEAPING LEARNER

THE LEAPING LEARNER

Exercise 51 – Definitions

Select the correct word for each of the following definitions. Each word can be used only once.

subdue	belligerent	gene	aspire	prominent
incision	dormant	famine	coincidence	grotesque

1. _____ : extreme scarcity of food in a country or large geographical area (noun)

2. _____ : to seek ambitiously for something of great or high value (verb)

3. _____ : a notable occurrence of two or more events at the same time by chance (noun)

4. _____ : to overpower or overcome by force (verb)

5. _____ : odd or unnatural in shape, appearance, or character (adj)

6. _____ : the basic physical unit of heredity (noun)

7. _____ : a cut or gash (noun)

8. _____ : an aggressively hostile demeanour (adj)

9. _____ : standing out so as to be seen easily (adj)

10. _____ : in a state of rest or inactivity (adj)

Exercise 52 – Synonyms

Choose one word from the five options which means the same or nearly the same as the bold word on the left.

1. **pledge**   agreement   breach   break   flail   degree

2. **fatal**   healthy   beneficial   whole   lethal   lightened

3. **dispute**   approve   design   alarm   putrid   quarrel

4. **gnarled**   straight   tardy   twisted   curt   stale

5. **radiant**   gloomy   bland   beaming   shameful   sparse

6. **dismayed**   discouraged   tall   jovial   leaning   sharp

7. **besieged**   reprieve   splendour   deranged   trapped   inspired

8. **habitat**   unnatural   tatty   dwelling   clothing   habit

9. **oppression**   blessing   opaque   opposite   injustice   powerful

10. **polite**   audacious   unpleasant   affable   confine   impressed

Riddle Time!

Q : Which word is the odd one out:
first, second, third, forth, fifth, sixth, seventh or eighth?

A : _Forth, is incorrectly spelled; it should be fourth._

Exercise 53 – Antonyms

Choose one word from the five options which means the opposite or nearly the opposite as the bold word on the left.

1. **potential**   probable   possible   unlikely   porter   anchored

2. **meek**   timid   savoured   linked   seek   bold

3. **apparent**   clear   obscure   great   brief   extra

4. **demean**   elevate   degrade   stale   mimic   matte

5. **compulsory**   forced   thrifty   pulse   distant   optional

6. **myriad**   multiple   mirror   limited   vexed   aromatic

7. **limber**   rigid   resilient   loathsome   lumber   fresh

8. **scowl**   grimace   spry   growl   smile   obtain

9. **forfeit**   gain   penalty   stroll   jam   stain

10. **indulge**   spoil   stark   oblige   divulge   deprive

Exercise 54 – Word connections

Three of the words in each list are connected to each other. Circle the word which does not belong.

1.   change   modify   alter   mimic

2.   heist   embezzlement   give   larceny

3.   brother   family   cousin   sister

4.   lemonade   espresso   cappuccino   tea

5.   necklace   gold   bracelet   ring

6.   hornet   bee   moth   wasp

7.   spear   gun   cannon   rifle

8.   lorry   motorcycle   airplane   van

9.   yellow   red   brown   blue

10.   entertain   seat   props   curtain

Who Is The Most Awesome Person Today ?

Exercise 55 – Find the Missing Word

Circle the word which would best fit into the sentence.

1. "What are you talking about?" my brother asked in a _____ way.
    copious   **substance**   **perplexed**   **dinky**

2. We should always _____ so that we can save for a rainy day.
    economise   **fret**   **squander**   **ponder**

3. Sal speaks many languages; she is able to _____ for tourists.
    diffuse   **pause**   **interpret**   **impede**

4. The shop assistant asked for a raise from her _____ salary.
    meagre   **substantial**   **ample**   **botched**

5. Pirates are known to _____ from ships.
    imply   **guzzle**   **ignite**   **plunder**

6. In some _____ areas, access to water is non-existent.
    rural   **privileged**   **refined**   **enticing**

7. The path leading to the beautiful property became _____ by overgrown bushes.
    thrifty   **compelled**   **concealed**   **obvious**

8. Jack _____ the bully by taking a shortcut instead of his usual route.
    soothed   **ranked**   **employed**   **eluded**

9. Unfortunately, his grades _____ at university when he stopped studying as much.
    rose   **plundered**   **plunged**   **deceived**

10.
    The boy was known to be extremely rude with _____ manners.
    magnificent   **ebullient**   **blithe**   **atrocious**

Exercise 56 – Similar Meanings

Fill in the missing letters to find the word with a similar meaning to the one in bold.

1. **belligerent**   agg __ __ s __ i __ e

2. **extinct**   di __ ap __ __ __ r

3. **hygienic**   sa __ it __ ry

4. **moral**   no __ __ e

5. **prosperous**   we __ l __ __ y

6. **symbol**   l __ g __

7. **moderate**   bal __ nc __ d

8. **diluted**   w __ __ ke __ __ d

9. **adhere**   __ be __

10. **community**   n __ i __ __ bou __ __ __ od

Exercise 57 – Opposite Meanings

Fill in the missing letters to find the word with the opposite meaning to the one in bold.

1. **fickle**   s __ ab __ e

2. **artificial**   n __ t __ r __ l

3. **belated**   pun __ tu __ __

4. **naive**   a __ a __ e

5. **flawed**   c __ rr __ __ t

6. **austere**   ex __ r __ v __ g __ n __

7. **replenish**   de __ let __

8. **ludicrous**   se __ s __ bl __

9. **elderly**   y __ __ th __ __ l

10. **communal**   i __ div __ __ __ a __

Exercise 58 – Pairs of Antonyms

Select the word from the box that is the antonym of the word on the left.

accept	consonant	tardy	omit	cowardice
hill	irrational	absent	incline	overt

1. vowel _____

2. include _____

3. logical _____

4. present _____

5. reject _____

6. heroism _____

7. early _____

8. decline _____

9. valley _____

10. concealed _____

Exercise 59 – Homophones

Circle the correct homophone to complete the sentence on the left.

1. She needed to send a _____ to pay for her rent this month.   **cheque**   **check**

2. Many children became very _____ during the lockdown.   **board**   **bored**

3. Dan needs self-raising _____ to make scones for tea.   **flower**   **flour**

4. I _____ him a care package in the post last week.   **scent**   **sent**

5. She learned how to _____ clothing as a new hobby.   **sew**   **sow**

6. The company needs to _____ new staff as soon as possible.   **higher**   **hire**

7. Sally felt rather _____ after having a long illness.   **weak**   **week**

8. I am not _____ to play video games before I finish my work.   **aloud**   **allowed**

9. After a busy day, I just want some _____ and quiet.   **piece**   **peace**

10. The tower stood strong _____ the earthquake.   **threw**   **through**

Riddle Time!

Q : What word doesn't belong in this group:
that, hat, what, mat, cat, sat, pat, or chat?

A : _What. It's pronounced differently; all of the others rhyme._

Exercise 60 – Compound Words

Circle one word from each set of brackets to form a compound word. The first part of the compound word will be in the first set of brackets.

1. (side   mean   flip)   (time   man   pass)   The word is _____.

2. (right   by   foot)   (end   print   left)   The word is _____.

3. (after   bin   star)   (noon   lean   town)   The word is _____.

4. (deep   friend   drop)   (ant   den   ship)   The word is _____.

5. (care   light   bet)   (full   taker   ten)   The word is _____.

6. (torch   talk   rain)   (storm   hood   worm)   The word is _____.

7. (leap   hand   cross)   (made   jump   port)   The word is _____.

8. (be   bar   lead)   (cause   can   way)   The word is _____.

9. (all   back   book)   (like   head   store)   The word is _____.

10. (wash   hand   band)   (room   bay   leap)   The word is _____.

Congratulations!

You have completed this vocabulary practice book!

Well done for learning so many new words and developing your vocabulary skills!

Have you come across any unfamiliar words in the last 10 exercises?
There is space below for you to write the words down, their definitions,
synonyms, and antonyms:

Word	Definition	Synonyms	Antonyms

THE LEAPING LEARNER   THE LEAPING LEARNER

Answers

Exercise 1 – Definitions

1. adhere
2. covert
3. orthodontics
4. lament
5. ignorant
6. fatigue
7. submissive
8. resort
9. perplexed
10. condemn

Exercise 2 – Synonyms

1. observe
2. depart
3. diminish
4. initiate
5. abhor
6. disclose
7. unruly
8. deceit
9. expire
10. pride

Exercise 3 – Antonyms

1. minuscule
2. soothed
3. calm
4. surrender
5. honesty
6. flourish
7. stable
8. clumsy
9. divulge
10. useful

Exercise 4 – Word connections

1. careful   ; the others are synonyms for 'irresponsible'
2. security   ; the others are synonyms for 'danger'
3. perilous   ; the others are synonyms for 'serenity'
4. lenient   ; the others are synonyms for 'steadfast'
5. restored   ; the others are synonyms for 'broken-down'
6. repel   ; the others are synonyms for 'entice'
7. lesson   ; the others are all words referring to the act of speaking or teaching
8. emotional   ; the others are synonyms for 'laid-back'
9. common   ; the others are synonyms for 'eccentric'
10. passivity   ; the others are synonyms for 'action'

Exercise 5 – Find the Missing Word

1. serial
2. charismatic
3. site
4. children's
5. cord
6. compliments
7. disassembled
8. coarse
9. lose
10. collage

Exercise 6 – Opposite Meanings

1. common
2. permanent
3. professional
4. awkward
5. boisterous
6. extravagant
7. unfortunate
8. scarce
9. liberate
10. response

Exercise 7 – Pairs of Synonyms

1. bloated
2. commodity
3. peddle
4. relish
5. callous
6. chore
7. confidential
8. onerous
9. shorten
10. roam

Exercise 8 – Word Categories

1. sanitary   – hygiene
2. fertile   – productive
3. regret   – sorrow
4. inhabitants – occupants
5. wretched   – tragic
6. emulate   – imitate
7. tranquil   – serene
8. trivial   – unimportant
9. deny   – forbid
10. flamboyant – dazzling

Exercise 9 – Similarities

1. disappeared
2. laborious
3. thoughtlessly
4. picturesque
5. determined
6. extradite
7. doubtful
8. genuine
9. appreciation
10. credible

Exercise 10 – Words Which Do Not Match

1. straighten
2. agitated
3. obscure
4. assist
5. silence
6. failure
7. evil
8. repel
9. shabby
10. release

Exercise 11 – Definitions

1. earmark
2. format
3. berate
4. novice
5. steadfast
6. pretend
7. ransack
8. primate
9. midriff
10. humdrum

Exercise 12 – Synonyms

1. appoint
2. blunt
3. tidy
4. sheltered
5. young
6. impassive
7. field
8. profit
9. sham
10. engage

Exercise 13 – Antonyms

1. damp
2. accept
3. intolerant
4. outdated
5. cover
6. frank
7. extraordinary
8. disorganised
9. expand
10. collect

Exercise 14 – Word Connections

1. charred   ; the other words mean 'anxious'
2. rural   ; the other words mean that something or someone has been cornered
3. murky   ; the other words are synonymous with 'clear'
4. ignited   ; the other words are synonyms for 'shabby'
5. delicious   ; the others mean 'tall'
6. quaint   ; the others are synonyms for 'permissive'
7. tranquil   ; the others are synonymous with 'famous'
8. youthful   ; the others are synonyms for 'irrational'
9. solid   ; the others are synonymous with 'confused'
10. obliged   ; the others are synonyms for 'foolish'

Exercise 15 – Find the Missing Word

1. course
2. advice
3. palate
4. vein
5. pact
6. mourning
7. manner
8. pedal
9. yolk
10. recede

Exercise 16 – Similar Meanings

1. sociable
2. crave
3. final
4. inadequate
5. suppress
6. unfold
7. conflict
8. careful
9. trait
10. wildfire

Exercise 17 – Opposite Meanings

1. help
2. delicate
3. resist
4. conventional
5. glossy
6. compliant
7. merciless
8. extreme
9. occupied
10. private

Exercise 18 – Homophones

1. knot
2. knead
3. peak
4. sense
5. reins
6. pear
7. yew
8. preys
9. site
10. towed

Exercise 19 – Similarities

1. depot
2. untidiness
3. solitude
4. distress
5. awakened
6. young
7. rough
8. shredded
9. perplexed
10. prisoners

Exercise 20 – Compound Words

1. waterfall
2. enterprise
3. bedrock
4. acceptable
5. backdrop
6. browsing
7. feather
8. supernatural
9. setback
10. nothing

Exercise 21 – Definitions

1. pigment
2. consent
3. meticulous
4. errand
5. asunder
6. inaugural
7. companion
8. tempestuous
9. plume
10. arduous

Exercise 22 – Synonyms

1. accept
2. extensive
3. falsify
4. esteemed
5. suppress
6. sociable
7. untouchable
8. excursion
9. betrayer
10. autonomy

Exercise 23 – Antonyms

1. doubt
2. gauche
3. often
4. ceasing
5. calm
6. affable
7. delightful
8. animosity
9. commence
10. demote

Exercise 24 – Find the Missing Word

1. renovated
2. fascinated
3. mediocre
4. precise
5. exhaustion
6. monotonous
7. sentimental
8. unsound
9. aversion
10. curtail

Exercise 25 – Similar Meanings

1. friendly
2. habitat
3. release
4. moist
5. communicate
6. brave
7. flash
8. remainder
9. well-spoken
10. speaker

Exercise 26 – Sorting Synonymous Words

1. simple – effortless, cinch, elementary, straightforward, basic, facile, uncomplicated, clear, plain, direct

2. complex – intricate, complicated, difficult, perplexing, arduous, challenging, involved, confusing, convoluted, elaborate

Exercise 27 – Pairs of Synonyms

1. sustain
2. permeate
3. defy
4. flippant
5. fluctuate
6. impartial
7. instinctive
8. imitate
9. bedlam
10. haughty

Exercise 28 – Word Categories

1. emerald – stone
2. architect – designer
3. beverage – drink
4. burrow – shelter
5. dialogue – conversation
6. cusine – cooking
7. saunter – walk
8. pedigree – ancestry
9. philanthropy – charity
10. adaptation – adjustment

Exercise 29 – Words Which Do Not Match

1. hire
2. silver
3. rib
4. raven
5. optimistic
6. learner
7. mayor
8. shed
9. vigilant
10. spoon

Exercise 30 – Double Meanings

1. aim
2. rock
3. lock
4. rule
5. behind
6. wind
7. function
8. mistake
9. hard
10. lie

Exercise 31 – Definitions

1. punctual
2. divinity
3. hoax
4. contract
5. pompous
6. admission
7. privilege
8. instantaneous
9. bargain
10. robust

Exercise 32 – Synonyms

1. panel
2. career
3. clothing
4. fake
5. distribution
6. gross
7. muffled
8. solemn
9. empty
10. trader

Exercise 33 – Antonyms

1. clarify
2. separate
3. harmonize
4. rational
5. release
6. ascend
7. organise
8. cruelty
9. affluent
10. inactivity

Exercise 34 – Word Connections

1. hospital   ; the others are types of professions
2. suffering   ; the others are synonyms for 'catastrophe' whereas 'suffering' is an emotional feeling
3. proclaim   ; the others are synonyms for 'promise'
4. artist   ; the others are tools used for art-making
5. bowl   ; the others are types of food/drink
6. sandals   ; the others are pieces of clothing worn in cold weather
7. wok   ; the others are cutlery
8. saunter   ; the others are ways of moving quickly
9. author   ; the others are pieces of writing
10. office   ; the others are places where people reside

Exercise 35 – Opposite Meanings

1. ordinary
2. mature
3. dependable
4. dehydrate
5. fragile
6. invisible
7. reasonable
8. destroy
9. unpleasant
10. tardy

Exercise 36 – Pairs of Antonyms

1. boycott
2. disturbance
3. uncouth
4. approval
5. melancholy
6. fulfilling
7. incautious
8. supreme
9. modest
10. convenient

Exercise 37 – Homophones

1. seam
2. draft
3. mousse
4. quarts
5. vial
6. dual
7. plum
8. bawled
9. stake
10. alter

Exercise 38 – Similarities

1. awoken
2. invaluable
3. worsened
4. cautioned
5. sickly
6. ardent
7. breakable
8. decayed
9. crafty
10. enhanced

Exercise 39 – Words Which Do Not Match

1. syrup
2. angry
3. external
4. waste
5. room
6. lazy
7. competent
8. uncover
9. mild
10. depth

Exercise 40 – Compound Words

1. passport
2. format
3. headline
4. ponytail
5. bookmark
6. anywhere
7. horseback
8. airplane
9. grandson
10. firefighter

Exercise 41 – Definitions

1. suggest
2. wholly
3. mere
4. immerse
5. vessel
6. grate
7. segregation
8. promote
9. odour
10. torment

Exercise 42 – Synonyms

1. antique
2. abolished
3. advantage
4. revenue
5. damage
6. austere
7. stiff
8. abscond
9. shy
10. group

Exercise 43 – Antonyms

1. rip-off
2. cruelty
3. dissuade
4. unintentional
5. dislike
6. enemy
7. order
8. suppress
9. continue
10. level

Exercise 44 – Find the Missing Word

1. constant
2. serene
3. emanated
4. keen
5. frugal
6. develop
7. flexible
8. parched
9. experienced
10. memorable

Exercise 45 – Similar Meanings

1. fierce
2. renew
3. clothes
4. arrangement
5. anger
6. structure
7. maximum
8. choice
9. plants
10. costly

Exercise 46 – Sorting Synonymous Words

1. light –   buoyant, dainty, agile, lightweight, luminosity, flimsy, slight, airy, floating, feathery

2. heavy –   hefty, substantial, weighty, considerable, massive, lead-footed, beefy, burdensome, dense, bulky

Exercise 47 – Word Categories

1. confusion   – uncertainty
2. mammal   – gorilla
3. ellipsis   – punctuation
4. dweller   – inhabitant
5. dialect   – accent
6. government – politics
7. orchid   – flower
8. brother   – sibling
9. wrench   – tool
10. lemon   – citrus

Exercise 48 – Similarities

1. forsake
2. lack
3. vegetation
4. deliberate
5. ordeal
6. vendors
7. household
8. punctured
9. aggravated
10. recounted

Exercise 49 – Words Which Do Not Match

1. hide
2. favourable
3. undermine
4. cherish
5. comfort
6. adjourn
7. repeal
8. depress
9. inflexible
10. crass

Exercise 50 – Double Meanings

1. race
2. mark
3. track
4. ditch
5. yield
6. direct
7. present
8. catch
9. content
10. mean

Exercise 51 – Definitions

1. famine
2. aspire
3. coincidence
4. subdue
5. grotesque
6. gene
7. incision
8. belligerent
9. prominent
10. dormant

Exercise 52 – Synonyms

1. agreement
2. lethal
3. quarrel
4. twisted
5. beaming
6. discouraged
7. trapped
8. dwelling
9. injustice
10. affable

Exercise 53 – Antonyms

1. unlikely
2. bold
3. obscure
4. elevate
5. optional
6. limited
7. rigid
8. smile
9. gain
10. deprive

Exercise 54– Word connections

1. mimic   ; the others are synonyms for 'difference'
2. give   ; the others are alternate words for 'theft'
3. family   ; the others are specific nouns for relatives
4. lemonade   ; the others are hot beverages
5. gold   ; the others are jewellery
6. moth   ; the others are insects which can sting
7. spear   ; the others are weapons which can fire ammunition
8. airplane   ; the others are modes of land transport
9. brown   ; the others are primary colours
10. entertain   ; the others are objects found within a theatre

Exercise 55 – Find the Missing Word

1. perplexed
2. economise
3. interpret
4. meagre
5. plunder
6. rural
7. concealed
8. eluded
9. plunged
10. atrocious

Exercise 56 – Similar Meanings

1. aggressive
2. disappear
3. sanitary
4. noble
5. wealthy
6. logo
7. balanced
8. weakened
9. obey
10. neighbourhood

Exercise 57 – Opposite Meanings

1. stable
2. natural
3. punctual
4. aware
5. correct
6. extravagant
7. deplete
8. sensible
9. youthful
10. individual

Exercise 58 – Pairs of Antonyms

1. consonant
2. omit
3. irrational
4. absent
5. accept
6. cowardice
7. tardy
8. incline
9. hill
10. overt

Exercise 59 – Homophones

1. cheque
2. bored
3. flour
4. sent
5. sew
6. hire
7. weak
8. allowed
9. peace
10. through

Exercise 60 – Compound Words

1. meantime
2. footprint
3. afternoon
4. friendship
5. caretaker
6. rainstorm
7. handmade
8. because
9. bookstore
10. washroom

Printed in Great Britain
by Amazon

61896481R00050